The
Justice
Gap

CONTENTS

CONTENTS

FIGURES AND TABLES

SUMMARY

1. This is the first discussion document issued by the independent Commission on Social Justice. It defines the values which will underpin the Commission's work, and documents the injustices that must be tackled if Britain is to be made a fairer society.

2. The term 'social justice' involves many ideas - including those of equality, need, entitlement, merit and desert. The purpose of our discussion here is to articulate widely held views about the character of our society, and to provide a framework of ideas within which to judge social and economic change. Most people say they believe in social justice, but their ideas are complex and indeterminate.

3. Our view of social justice consists of a hierarchy of four key ideas, starting with a consensual proposition and proceeding to a radical one. Our four principles of social justice are:

   The foundation of a free society is the equal worth of all citizens.

   All citizens are entitled, as a right of citizenship, to be able to meet their basic needs - for income, food, shelter, education and health.

   Self-respect and personal autonomy are inherent in the idea of equal worth, but their fulfilment depends on the widest possible access to opportunities and life-chances.

   Inequalities are not necessarily unjust - but those which are should be reduced and where possible eliminated.

4. These four ideas are the basis of the objectives for public policy set out in our second report, *Social Justice in a Changing World*. They also set standards by which the social and economic structure of the UK can be judged. That is the purpose of the 'New Map of Injustice' in Part 3 of this report, which examines the extent to which the UK lives up to these four principles of social justice. Our evidence reveals a profound 'justice gap' in Britain today.

5. **Equal Worth of all Citizens**

Virtually everyone believes in equality of *something*, and most countries claim to treat all citizens equally. It is widely recognised that fundamental political and human rights are the basis of a civil society. In the UK every citizen has rights to vote, to a fair trial and to freedom of association. For some people, however, these formal rights mean little: for example, one in ten UK citizens are not registered to vote, and access to the law is being limited by cuts in Legal Aid.

6. **Basic Needs**

For 'equal worth' to be meaningful, people must be able to meet their needs, or at least their basic needs. The welfare state was designed fifty years ago to help all citizens secure a minimum standard of living. For most people, this has been achieved. But for a significant minority, basic needs are not met: there are 400,000 people officially registered as homeless in Britain today; one in five people live on or below the poverty line; and one in five 21-year olds are innumerate.

7. **Opportunities and Life-Chances**

Self-respect and equal citizenship demand more than the meeting of basic needs. They demand the opportunities and life-chances central to personal freedom and autonomy. Opportunities and life-chances in the UK are heavily skewed towards an elite and are limited by the chance of birth. For instance, while nine in ten children aged under five in Cleveland have a chance of a place in a nursery or primary school, fewer than one in six do in Bromley. Three-quarters of school leavers fail to get two A levels, and two-thirds of adult workers have no qualifications at all.

8.   Unjust Inequalities

We do not claim that all inequalities are unjust. In fact, few people believe that arithmetic equality is either feasible or desirable. But structural inequalities of power and position such as discrimination or abuse of power in the labour market are unjust. The faster rise in the salaries of top executives, compared to the average worker, has, over the last five years, added £200,000 to their pay packets. These large increases have not been associated with successful company performance; if anything, the opposite is true.

9.   The Beveridge report of 1942 aimed to eradicate the 'five great evils' of want, ignorance, disease, squalor and idleness. As our New Map of Injustice shows, this project remains to be completed for a significant minority of citizens. It must now, however, be supplemented by a new agenda - the extension of the 'five great opportunities' which provide the basis for individual fulfilment and national renewal. The extension of these opportunities will provide an important focus for the Commission's work in the months ahead. The five great opportunities are:

Lifelong Learning

Social reform and economic progress now depend on the skills and talents of the majority of citizens, and not just those of the few. Opportunities for learning must be extended, not simply for children, but for all citizens throughout their lives.

Work

The opportunity to work is central to personal identity as well as the nation's economic and social life. We need to extend new opportunities for employment to all who want it, while ensuring that unpaid work is properly valued.

Good Health

While the NHS was founded on the provision of treatment for the sick, the achievement of health potential depends on the promotion of good health - at home, at work and in the community.

Safe Environment

Our environment affects us all, regardless of wealth. For example, crime and the fear of crime, both on the increase, severely restrict freedom and well-being.

Financial Independence

Welfare benefits can provide for minimum needs, but at current levels do not offer financial independence. Independence is founded on the opportunity for a secure lifetime income and the capacity to save.

10. Some people regard equality of opportunity as a weak form of equality: and some support it for that reason. If we look seriously at the distribution of life-chances in our society, we cannot help but regard a commitment to the extension of opportunities as a radical doctrine, and one that lies at the heart of social justice.

1
INTRODUCTION

The future of welfare - the NHS and education as well as national insurance and social security benefits - is now at the forefront of the political agenda. Fifty years after the publication of William Beveridge's report, *Social Insurance and Allied Services*, it is increasingly clear that the institutions and policies established by the 1945 Labour Government are no longer adequate. The UK needs a vision of social and economic progress as coherent and compelling for the beginning of the 21st century as Beveridge's was for the second half of the 20th.

In December 1992, the Leader of the Labour Party, John Smith MP, established the independent Commission on Social Justice under the auspices of the Institute for Public Policy Research (IPPR). His initiative was promptly followed by the Government's announcement of their own review of public spending, taxation and benefits. In the last few months, a series of leaks about possible reforms - charges for hospital visits, restrictions in invalidity benefit, the end of free prescriptions for the elderly - have prompted a furious debate among politicians, campaigners and commentators. Although the social security budget alone now totals nearly £80 billion, no-one is satisfied. People who depend upon benefits have too little to live on; proposals for extra spending seem to fly in the face of the public sector borrowing requirement and the apparent reluctance of taxpayers to pay more; and welfare spending cannot keep pace with the effects of economic failure - mass unemployment, low pay and poverty.

Government ministers respond to attacks on their own review by pointing to this Commission as evidence of the need for tough choices: tax increases, expenditure cuts, or both. But there are fundamental differences between the Government's review and this Commission's work. It is not only that our work is public, designed to engage as many people and organisations as possible. We are interested in actively promoting social justice; the government are interested simply in saving money. We start from the proposition that, in contrast to the prevailing ideology of the 1980s, economic and social policy are not separate, but interdependent; wealth and welfare go hand in hand.

The problems of the welfare state stem from profound structural changes in our economy, our society and our politics - changes which are mirrored in other industrialised countries but which take a particular form in Britain. The three pillars of the Beveridge model - full (male) employment, the nuclear family, and a strong state - can no longer be taken for granted. Shifts in the labour market, families and the welfare state are inter-connected: changes in one area affect the others, and none can be reformed alone. In our second discussion paper, *Social Justice in a Changing World*, we analyse these structural changes and make preliminary suggestions about what the objectives of reform should be. Our first task here, however, is to clarify the values at the foundation of our enquiry.

The immediate question facing the Commission at its first meeting stemmed from our title. There are many ideas of 'social justice', and we have had to develop our own understanding of the term. Public policy is never value-free, and it is as well to be clear about its purpose from the outset. In Part 2 of this publication, we therefore set out a preliminary conceptual framework for thinking about issues of social justice. We are not trying to develop a theoretical model that neatly answers specific questions of public policy: ideas of social justice cannot tell us how much unemployment benefit or the pension should be, but they can provide a framework of values to evaluate policy options. As Professor Michael Kelly of Southampton University put it to us: 'unless they have a moral dimension, the Commission's proposals will lack the passion and conviction necessary to sustain sufficient impetus'.

At the outset of our enquiry, however, it is important to emphasise two very large restrictions on our work. With certain exceptions, we cannot hope to extend our considerations very far beyond the borders of the United Kingdom, or very far into the future. We live in what in global terms is a well-off country, spared the extreme deprivation suffered in large parts of the world. International injustice, notwithstanding the fact that its horror dwarfs the arguments that take place within the industrialised world, is not our primary concern: our focus is on justice and injustice within the UK. Where relations with other countries involve questions of justice and injustice, the Commission will have to proceed on the assumption that this is one area which we will not be able to address adequately. The UK is, however, a member of the European Community, and we will therefore be concerned with policy developments at the European level.

Equally, the Commission cannot hope to consider in detail ecological questions of what we should provide and save for posterity. We are, nonetheless, very much aware of the ecological constraints on economic development, and will take into account the urgent need for adequate conservation and ecological protection in making our own recommendations. We cannot, however, deal with all the issues raised by the principle of sustainable development.

The next section of this report sets out our conceptual framework. Part 3 then examines how Britain fares according to the standards set in Part 2. The nature and extent of social injustice has changed over the last fifty years, and our 'New Map of Injustice' is designed to examine the gap between our ideas of social justice and the realities of life in Britain today. Part 4 then sets out what we believe to be the new agenda for public policy in Britain - an attempt to take forward the attack on the 'five great evils' identified by Beveridge, by identifying 'five great opportunities' which provide the basis for social reform and economic renewal in the years ahead.

2
WHAT IS SOCIAL JUSTICE?

a priori

In deciding to develop a conceptual framework for thinking about social justice, the Commission made a big assumption, namely that there is such a thing as 'social justice'. Some people (particularly of the libertarian Right) deny that there is a worthwhile idea of *social* justice at all. They say that justice is an idea confined to the law, with regard to crime, punishment, and the settling of disputes before the courts. They claim that it is nonsense to talk about resources in society being fairly or unfairly distributed. The free market theorist, F.A. Hayek, for example, argued that the process of allocating wealth and property 'can be neither just nor unjust, because the results are not intended or foreseen, and depend on a multitude of circumstances not known in their totality to anybody'.

What libertarians really mean, however, is not that there is no such thing as social justice, but rather that there is only one criterion of a just outcome in society, namely that it should be the product of a free market. But this is not as simple as it may sound, because ideas of fairness (and not merely of efficiency) are themselves used in defining what counts as a free market. While it is often said that a given market competition is not fair because it is not being played 'on a level field', it is not clear what counts as levelling the field, as opposed to altering the result of the match. For example, anti-trust laws can be seen as an interference in a free market, or a device for making the field level.

doubt hmm

In fact, people in modern societies *do* have strong ideas about social justice. We all know this from daily conversation, and opinion polls regularly confirm it. We are confident that at least in our belief that there is such a thing as 'social justice', we reflect the common sense of the vast majority of people. However, polls are not easy to interpret, and they make it clear that people's ideas about social justice are complex.

There is more than one notion associated with the term social justice. In some connections, for example, justice is thought to have something to do with *equality*. Sometimes it seems to relate to *need*: for example, it can seem notably unfair if bad fortune prevents someone from having something they really need, such as medical care, less unfair if it is something they just happen to want. Yet again, justice relates to such notions as *entitlement*, *merit*, and *desert*. These are not the same as each other. For example, if someone wins the prize in the lottery, they are entitled to the money, and it would be unjust to take it away from them, but it has nothing to do with their merits, and they have done nothing to deserve it. Similarly, if talented people win prizes in an activity that requires no great practice or effort, they are entitled to the prize and get it on the strength of their merits (as opposed, for instance, to someone's getting it because he is the son of the promoter), but they may well have not done anything much to deserve it. People who are especially keen on the notion of desert may want there to be prizes only for effort; or, at least, think that prizes which command admiration (as the lottery prize does not) should be awarded only for effort. Humanity has shown so far a steady reluctance to go all the way with this view.

As well as being *complex* in this way, people's views about justice are also *indeterminate*. This means that it is often unclear what the just outcome should be - particularly when various considerations of social justice seem to pull in different directions, as they often do. Most people, for instance, think that inheritance is at least not intrinsically evil, and that parents are entitled to leave property to their children. But no-one thinks that one can leave anything one likes to one's children - one's job, for instance - and almost everyone thinks that it can be just for the state to tax inheritances in order to deal with social injustice, or simply to help the common good.

The mere fact that people's ideas about justice are both complex and indeterminate has an important consequence for democratic politics. There is more than one step from general ideas to practical recommendations. There have to be *general* policies directed to social justice, and these are going to be at best an interpretation of people's ideas on such matters. General policies will hope to offer considerations which people can recognise as making sense in the light of their own experience and ideas (this need not exclude challenging some of those ideas.) *Specific* policies, however, involve a further step, since they have to express general policies in a particular administrative form. A given scheme of taxation or social security is, in that sense, at two removes from the complex and indeterminate ideas that are its moral roots.

This is not to deny that some administrative practices may acquire a symbolic value of their own. In the 1940s, the death grant was a symbol of society's commitment to end paupers' funerals and ensure for every family the means to offer deceased relatives a proper burial. It is a matter of acute political judgement to decide whether one is dealing with an important example of such a value, as opposed to a fetish (in the more or less literal sense of an inert object that has been invested with value that does not belong to it in its own right.) Not every arrangement that has been taken to be an essential embodiment of social justice is, in changing circumstances, really so.

Theories of Social Justice

There are important theories of social justice. The most ambitious give a general account of what social justice is, explain and harmonise the relations between the different considerations associated with it, do the same for the relations between justice and other goods, notably liberty, help to resolve apparent conflicts between different values, and in the light of all that, even give pointers to practical policies. The most famous such theory in modern discussion is that of John Rawls, which gives a very rich elaboration to a very simple idea: that the fair division of a cake would be one that could be agreed on by people who did not know which piece they were going to get.

Rawls invokes an 'Original Position', in which representatives of various parties to society are behind 'a veil of ignorance' and do not know what role each party will occupy in the society. They are asked to choose a general scheme for the ordering of society. The scheme that they would reasonably choose in these imagined circumstances constitutes, on Rawls' view, the scheme of a just society.

Rawls' theory, and others with similar aims, contain important insights, and anyone who is trying to think about these problems should pay attention to them. But there is an important question - one acknowledged by Rawls himself - of what relation such a theory can have to politics. Rawls thinks that his theory articulates a widely-spread sense of fairness, but it is certain that the British public would not recognise in such a theory, or in any other with such ambitions, all its conflicting ideas and feelings about social justice. Even if the Commission, improbably, all agreed on Rawls's or some other such theory, we would not be justified in presenting our conclusions in terms of that theory. The Commission has a more practical purpose.

Our task is to find compelling ways of making our society more just. We shall be able to do so only if we think in ways that people can recognise and respect about such questions as how best to understand merit and need; how to see the effects of luck in different spheres of life; what is implied in saying, or denying, that health care is a morally special kind of good which makes a special kind of demand.

The Commission has to guard against all or nothing assumptions. It is not true that either we have a complete top-down theory, or we are left only with mere prejudice and subservience to polls. This particularly applies to conflict. Confronted, as will often be the case, with an apparent conflict within justice, or between justice and some other value, we may tend to assume that there are only two possibilities: the conflict is merely apparent, and we should understand liberty and equality (for instance) in such a way that they cannot conflict; or it is a real conflict, and then it can only be left to politics, majorities, subjective taste, or whatever. This will not do. Reflection may not eliminate all conflicts, but it can help us to understand them, and then arrive at policy choices.

The Equal Worth of Every Citizen

Social justice is often thought to have something specially to do with equality, but this idea, in itself, determines very little. A basic question is: equality of what? Furthermore, not all inequalities are unjust. For example, what people can do with money varies. Thus disabled people may well need more resources to reach a given quality of life than other people do, and if you are trying to be fair to people with regard to the quality of their life, unequal amounts of money is what fairness itself will demand. What this shows, as the philosopher and economist Amartya Sen has insisted, is that equality in one dimension goes with inequality in another. Since people have different capacities to turn resources into worthwhile activity (for instance because they are disabled), people will need different resources to be equally capable of worthwhile activity.

In fact, virtually everyone in the modern world believes in equality of *something*. All modern states are based on belief in some sort of equality and claim to treat their citizens equally. But what is involved in 'treating people equally'? Minimally, it implies political and civil liberties, equal rights before the law, equal protection against arbitrary arrest, and so forth. These things provide the basis of a 'civil society', a society of equal citizens.

However, these rights and freedoms cannot stand by themselves. More than this formal level of equality is needed if the minimal demands themselves are to be properly met. It is a familiar point that equality before the law does not come to much if one cannot afford a good lawyer. The 'equal freedom' of which modern democratic states boast should amount to more (as Anatole France observed) than the freedom to sleep on park benches and under bridges. Everyone needs the means to make use of their equal freedom, which otherwise would be hollow. Formal equalities have substantive consequences. Perhaps the most basic question about the nature of social justice in a modern society is what those substantive consequences are.

Meeting Basic Needs

People are likely to be restricted in what they can do with their freedom and their rights if they are poor, or ill, or lack the education which, to a greater extent today than ever before, is the basis of employment opportunities, personal fulfilment, and people's capacities to influence what happens to them. These concerns define areas of *need*, and it is a natural application of the idea that everyone is of equal worth that they should have access to what they need, or at least to what they basically need.

Some basic needs are met by providing resources, or by helping people to save or acquire resources. This is the case with paid work; with financial security in old age; and with provisions for dealing with lack of resources, such as benefit in case of unemployment. In the case of health care and education, however, the most appropriate way of meeting needs seems to be not through money, but in kind; we think that someone who is ill has a right to access to treatment for their illness, but not that they have a right to funds which they can choose to spend on treatment or not. One way of expressing this commitment is that the state should itself provide the service. Another is that the state should provide means which command health care or education, but which cannot be converted into money. In the case of health, this may take the form of public insurance, though this can raise basic questions of fairness (with regard to individual risk) as well as of efficiency.

The case of health now raises a fundamental question which was not present fifty years ago. Health care has always seemed a very special good, in relation to social justice as in other respects. It involves our most basic interests, gives great power to certain professionals, and carries heavy symbolic value (brought out, for instance, in Richard Titmuss' famous discussion of blood donation *The Gift Relationship*). Treating health as one commodity, to be bought and sold like any other, is found offensive in most parts of the world (and Americans, though used to that attitude, seem to be turning against it.) Our sentiments about health care merge with our sense of some very basic obligations: most people feel that resources should be used to save an identified person (as opposed to a merely statistical casualty) from death.

But today it is a fact that medicine's resources to extend life are expanding at an accelerating rate, and so is their cost. This raises hard questions not only about the distribution of resources devoted to health care (who gets the kidney machine?), but also about the amount of resources that should be devoted to health care at all. These hard questions are questions of justice, among other things. Confronted with the opportunity to save someone in the street from death, we will think that we should stop to save them even if the cost is not taking the children to school, but is it fair to save every saveable person from death at the cost of sending many children to quite inadequate schools?

To answer these questions, the Commission will need to consider what *sort* of goods we take health and health care to be. This was a less pressing question in the past, but it is now harder to avoid the issue of what we are distributing when we distribute medical care, and of what we most want it to do.

Education is also a good to which everyone has a right, because it is so closely tied to basic needs, to personal development, and to one's role in society. But it is also connected to equality in another way. Disadvantage is, notoriously, inherited, and an unfair situation in one generation tends to mean an unfair start for the next. Educational opportunity is still what it always has been, a crucial means for doing something about this unfairness.

This brings out a further point, that the ideal of 'equality of opportunity', which has often been thought by reformers to be a rather weak aspiration, is in fact very radical, if it is taken seriously. The changes required in order to give the most disadvantaged in our society the same life-chances as the more fortunate would be very wide-ranging indeed.

Opportunities and Life-Chances

Self-respect and equal citizenship demand more than the meeting of basic needs for income, shelter and so on. They demand the opportunities and life-chances central to personal freedom and autonomy. In a commercial society (outside monasteries, kibbutzim, etc.), self-respect standardly requires a certain amount of personal property. As Adam Smith remarked, a working man in 18th century Scotland needed to own a decent linen shirt as a condition of self-respect, even though that might not be true of every man everywhere.

This does not mean that Adam Smith's man should be issued with a shirt. In a commercial society, his need is rather for the resources to buy a shirt of his choice. This is connected with his needing it as a matter of self-respect, which suggests something else, namely that where resources are supplied directly, for instance to those who are retired or who are caring for members of their families, it must be in ways which affirm their self-respect. But most people, for most of their lives, want the opportunities to earn the resources for themselves. The obvious question is whether everyone therefore has a right to a job, or the right to the means to gain a job.

The trouble, clearly, is that it may not be in the power of government directly to bring this about. Having a job, at least as the world is now, is closely connected with self-respect and hence with the equality of citizens, and for this as well as other reasons it must be a high priority for any government to create the circumstances in which there are jobs for those who want them. To insist, however, on a right to work - a right, presumably, which each person holds against the government - may not be the best way of expressing this aim. The Commission will therefore consider not only ways in which employment may be increased, but also what provision social justice demands for those who are unable to do paid work, or who are engaged in valuable unpaid work, or when significant levels of unemployment persist, even for a temporary period. Tackling unemployment is, of course, central to the realisation of social justice.

There are questions here of how resources and opportunities can be extended to the unemployed. But there is a wider question as well, that extends to the provision for other needs: how opportunities may be created for the expression of people's autonomy and the extension of their freedom to determine their own lives. There is no doubt that advocates of social justice have often been insensitive to this dimension. The designers of the welfare state wanted to put rights in the place of charity: the idea of *entitlement* to benefit was meant to undercut any notion that the better-off were doing the worse-off a good turn. But the entitlement was often still understood as an entitlement to be given or issued with certain goods and services, the nature of which it was, in many cases, the business of experts to determine. There is a much greater awareness today that what people need is the chance to provide for themselves: as we will stress in our second publication, 'there is a limit to what government can do for people, but there is no limit to what they can be enabled to achieve for themselves'.

Relatedly, there is a stronger sense today that the aims of social justice are served not only by redistribution, by bringing resources after the event to people who have done badly. Social justice requires as well that structures should be adapted and influenced in ways that can give more people a better chance in the first place. That is why opportunities, and breaking down barriers to them, are so important.

There are, without doubt, conflicts between these various considerations. You cannot both encourage people's freedom to live their own lives as they choose, and guarantee that they will not suffer if they do not live them well. You cannot both allow people to spend money, if they wish, on their children's education - a right that exists in every democratic country - and also bring it about that everyone gets exactly the same education whether they pay privately for it or not. Here there are questions, too, of how far publicly supported provision to meet need should aim only at a minimal level, available to those without other provision, and how far it should seek to provide a high level of service for everyone. The view of most people is probably that the first answer applies to some needs and the goods and services that meet them, while in the case of health care and education, at least, no-one should be excluded by disadvantage from a very high level of provision. Exactly how those different aims should now be conceived, and the extent to which they can realistically be carried out, are central questions for the Commission.

Unjustified Inequalities

Proponents of equality sometimes seem to imply that *all* inequalities are unjust (although they usually hasten to add that they are not in fact arguing for 'arithmetical equality'.) We do not accept this. It seems fair, for instance, that a medical student should receive a lower income than the fully qualified doctor; or that experience or outstanding talent should be rewarded, and so on. Different people may have different views about what the basis of differential rewards should be; but most people accept, as we do, that some inequalities are just. There is, however, a question about the justifiable *extent* of an inequality, even if we accept that the inequality *per se* is not unjust.

Similarly, most people believe that it is fair for people to bequeath their property as they see fit, even though this means that some will inherit more then others. Nonetheless, it is also accepted that society may claim a share of an inheritance through the taxation of wealth or gifts, particularly when the estate is large. It is, after all, offensive to most ideas of social justice that a growing number of people own two homes while others have nowhere to live at all. This does not imply that one person's property should be confiscated to house another; but it does suggest the need for a fundamental reform of housing policy, an issue the Commission will certainly be addressing.

But if some inequalities are just, it is obviously the case that not all are so. It would, for instance, be unjust to allow people to inherit jobs from their parents: employment should be open to all, on the basis of merit. Inheritance of a family title offends many people's views about a classless society, but could not be said to deny somebody else something which they deserved. But inheritance of a peerage, in the UK, carries with it automatic entitlement to a seat and vote in the Second Chamber of Parliament: and that is an inequality of power which seems manifestly unjust.

Entitlement and Desert

Parents can, however, pass on intelligence, talent, charm and other qualities, as well as property or titles. Rawls in his theory rests a lot on the fact that a person's talents, and his or her capacity to make productive use of those talents, are very much matters of luck and are also, in some part, the product of society. Nobody, he has rightly insisted, *deserves* his or her (natural) talents. From this he has inferred that nobody, at a level of basic principle, deserves the rewards of his or her talents. He argues that no-one has a right to something simply because it is the product of his or her talents, and society has a right to redistribute that product in accordance with the demands of social justice.

This is a very strong and surprising claim. Some people might agree that no-one deserves a reward that they get on the basis of some raw advantage, without any investment of effort. (Of course, given the existing rules, that does not mean that they are not entitled to it, or that it can merely be taken away from them. It means that it would not necessarily be an injustice to change the rules.) But those who agree to this are very likely to think that people who *do* invest effort deserve its rewards, at least up to a certain point. But Rawls's argument applies just as much to effort as to raw talent. First, it is practically impossible to separate the relative contributions of effort and talent to a particular product. Moreover, the capacity to make a given degree of effort is itself not equally distributed, and may plausibly be thought to be affected by upbringing, culture and other social factors. Virtually everything about a person that yields a product is itself undeserved. So no rewards, on Rawls's view, are, at the most basic level, a matter of desert.

Few people believe this. If someone has taken a lot of trouble in designing and tending a garden, for instance, they will be proud of it, and appropriately think of its success as theirs. The same applies to many aspects of life. This does suggest that there is something wrong with the idea that basically people never earn anything by their talents or labours - that in the last analysis all that anyone's work represents is a site at which society has achieved something. Yet, certainly, one does not 'deserve' the talents of birth. It must be true, then, that one can deserve the rewards of one's talents without deserving one's talents. As the American philosopher Robert Nozick forcefully put it, why does desert 'have to go all the way down'?

What the various arguments about entitlement and desert suggest seems to be something close to what many people believe: that there is basic justice in people having some differential reward for their productive activities, but that they have no right to any *given* differential of their reward over others. It is not simply self-interest, or again scepticism about government spending programmes (though that is certainly a factor), that makes people resist the idea that everyone's income is in principle a resource for redistribution; that idea also goes against their sense of what is right. They rightly think that redistribution of income is not an aim in itself.

At the same time, they acknowledge that the needs of the less fortunate make a claim. Luck is everywhere, and one is entitled to some rewards of luck, but there are limits to this entitlement when one lives and works with other people. Even if one is entitled to some rewards from the product of one's efforts and talents, there is the further point that in a complex enterprise such as a company or family, there is rarely a product which is solely and definitely the product of a given person's efforts and talents.

This is no doubt one reason why people are sceptical about vast rewards to captains of industry. It is also a question of the relation of one person's activity to that of others. Few people mind that Pavarotti or Lenny Henry are paid large sums - there is only one of them, and they are undoubtedly the star of the show. But in some cases, one person's reward can be another person's loss. The Nobel Prize winning economist Professor James Meade argued in a submission to the Commission that 'Keynesian full-employment policy ... collapsed simply and solely because a high level of money expenditures came to lead not to a high level of output and employment but to a high rate of money wages, costs and prices...It is very possible that to absorb two million extra workers into employment would require a considerable reduction in real wage costs.'

This raises a crucial point, concerning the power to determine one's own rewards, and the relationship of that power to questions of justice and desert. In contrast to a simple focus on the distribution of rewards, this raises the question of the *generation* of rewards, the processes whereby inequalities are generated.

Unequal incomes are inherent in a market economy. Even if everyone started off with the same allocation of money, differences would soon emerge. Not all labour commands the same price; not all investments produce the same return; some people work longer hours, others prefer more leisure, and so on. The resulting inequalities are not necessarily unjust - although the extent of them may be. In the real world, of course, people start off with very different personal and financial resources. The problem is that too many of these inequalities are exacerbated in the UK's system of market exchange.

But market economies are not all of a piece; different kinds of market produce different outcomes. For instance, Germany, Japan and Sweden all have more equal earnings distributions than the UK, where the gap between the highest and lowest paid is wider today than at any time since 1886. Social justice therefore has a part to play in deciding how a market is constructed, and not simply with the end result.

Fair Reward

Most people have some idea of a 'fair reward'. For example, it is clear to the vast majority of people that disadvantage and discrimination on grounds of sex or race or disability is unjust. However, once one gets beyond the general idea, there is less agreement on what fair rewards should be. Even if there were more agreement about this, it is very difficult, both practically and morally, to impose such notions on a modern economy. The very idea of a society that can be effectively managed from the top on the basis of detailed centralised decisions is now discredited. Moreover, our society does not stand by itself and happily does not have walls around it, and people can go elsewhere.

Ideas of social justice in this area are not, however, necessarily tied to the model of a command economy. It is often clear, at least, that given rewards in a market economy are not fair, because they are not being determined by such things as talent, effort, and the person's contribution to the enterprise, but rather by established power relations. Real life does not conform to economic models: people are not paid for the 'marginal product' of their labour. They are paid, among other things, according to social norms. In one sense, such distortions are the product of the market: they are what we get if market processes, uncorrected, are allowed to reflect established structures and habits of power. Examples of this are the huge salaries and bonuses distributed to the directors of some large companies. As the next section of this report clearly shows, these salaries and bonuses are often quite unrelated to the performance of the company concerned, and are sometimes actually inversely correlated with company performance.

In another sense, unjust inequalities are themselves distortions of the market: it is not a fair market in talent and effort if it is not talent and effort that determine the outcome. This is most obviously demonstrated in the case of inequalities of pay between men and women. Although the 1970 Equal Pay Act eliminated overt pay inequities, it had a limited effect on the gap between men's and women's pay, which resulted in the main from job segregation and gender-biased views of what different jobs and different qualities were worth. Hence the concept of 'equal pay for work of equal value', which permits comparisons between two very different jobs performed for the same employer. Although designed to eradicate gender as a consideration in earnings, equal value claims may in practice require a complete transformation in an organisation's pay-setting. Equal pay for work of equal value, after all, implies unequal pay for work of unequal value: thus, the basis for differentials has to be made explicit and justified.

Different organisations and people will have different views of what constitutes a fair basis for differentials: it should not be an aim of government to substitute its own view of fair wage settlements. It is, however, a legitimate aim of policy concerned with social justice to develop social institutions (of which equal value laws are one example) which will enable people to express their own ideas of a fair reward.

The Meaning of Social Justice: A Summary

In arriving at our principles of social justice, we reject the view, so fashionable in the 1980s, that human beings are simply selfish individuals, for whom there is 'no such thing as society'. People are essentially social creatures, dependent on one another for the fulfilment of their needs and potential, and willing to recognise their responsibilities to others as well as claiming their rights from them. We believe our four principles of social justice, based on a basic belief in the intrinsic worth of every human being, echo the deeply-held views of many people in this country. They provide a compelling justification and basis for our work:

1.   The foundation of a free society is the equal worth of all citizens.

2.   Everyone is entitled, as a right of citizenship, to be able to meet their basic needs.

3.   The right to self-respect and personal autonomy demands the widest possible spread of opportunities.

4.   Not all inequalities are unjust, but unjust inequalities should be reduced and where possible eliminated.

This summary completes the description of our conceptual framework for thinking about ideas of social justice. We have attempted to articulate some widely-held feelings about the character of our society and to describe them in a way that makes sense.

Our next task is to examine the extent to which Britain today meets the standards of social justice set out in this publication so far.

3
A NEW MAP OF INJUSTICE

We have set out in some detail the principles of social justice which the Commission has adopted. This part of the document is about *injustice* - the extent to which the UK today fails to recognise civil and political rights, meet basic needs, expand opportunities, and limit unjustifiable inequalities. The Map of Injustice described here will dramatise the extent of the 'justice gap' between ideas of justice and the realities of injustice. The Map defines the nature and scope of the Commission's task in our attempt to develop proposals to make Britain a more socially just society.

The Equal Worth of Every Citizen

The foundation of our conception of social justice is the equal worth of all citizens. 'Equal worth' is most obviously enshrined in civil and political rights - equality before the law, universal suffrage, freedom of association, for example - that are the birthright of all citizens in a free community. Although the Commission was not set up to consider civil and political rights or, more generally, constitutional reform, it is important to indicate how far Britain measures up to human rights principles: important not only because these rights are the starting point for our view of social justice, but also because of the close link between some civil and political rights and the economic and social opportunities with which we are centrally concerned.

In theory, the UK grants full civil and political rights to all citizens (although the definition of citizenship has itself become considerably more restrictive over the last decade). One positive example is that the UK, unlike France and Germany, offers full citizenship with voting rights to all legal immigrants. However, theory and practice often fail to match up.

In terms of political rights:

● One in ten of the UK's citizens are not registered to vote. For ethnic minorities the figures are more disturbing still: one in seven Asians and one in four Afro-Caribbeans are not on the electoral register.

● Many disabled people are not able to vote; the Spastics Society found that only 12 per cent of polling stations at the last election presented no problems of access for disabled people. Many disabled people do not want to use postal or proxy votes.

● Local democracy has been shorn of much of its meaning by the centralisation of power at Westminster through the 80s. The Commission has heard how in some wards turnout in local elections can be as low as 16 per cent. Because community organisations often hold out greater hope for change, turnout in elections for their committees is sometimes higher than in local elections.

In terms of human rights, there is also a gap between theory and practice. The UK government has lost more cases in the European Court of Human Rights than any other country. At present, however, a human rights case can take 10 years to reach the European court, and reforms to speed up the processing of human rights cases are being stalled by the UK. The enactment of Clause 28 of the 1988 Local Government Act - banning Local Authorities from the 'promotion of homosexuality' or the teaching of the 'acceptability of homosexuality as a pretended family relationship' - fostered a climate of fear and distrust, and was a step backwards from key values of tolerance and civil liberty.

Freedom of association and, specifically, the right to join a trade union, is protected by the European Human Rights Convention and other instruments of international law. The present Government claims to accept the principle that no-one should be victimised or discriminated against for joining a union, although they continue to deny union membership rights to civil servants employed at GCHQ. A recent case illustrates how fragile the right to join a union actually is. In April 1993, the Court of Appeal ruled in two cases - involving an NUJ member at the *Daily Mail* and TGWU members employed by Associated British Ports at Southampton Docks - that employers were not entitled to discriminate against union members by offering higher pay to employees who renounced a collective agreement in favour of a personal contract.

That clear ruling, however, is being overturned by the Government in a last-minute amendment to the Trade Union Reform and Employment Rights Bill - an amendment which has been condemned, among others, by former Conservative Employment Minister, Peter Bottomley MP.

In theory, the UK guarantees equality before the law. In practice, however, not everyone can afford the price of justice. Restrictions on Legal Aid introduced in April 1993 mean that, according to Law Society estimates, the number of people eligible for civil Legal Aid has fallen by about one third.

● The Law Society says that the changes 'represent the most serious threat to access to justice since Legal Aid was introduced over 40 years ago.' The changes mean that litigants who would, for example, previously have paid £51 will now be expected to find £300-400. For many who are just above the income support level (the new eligibility line for free Legal Aid) legal costs are proving prohibitive.

There is also strong evidence of inconsistency in sentencing on ethnic lines. The most recent definitive study shows that a black offender is 17 per cent more likely to receive a custodial sentence than a white offender.

In theory the UK offers its citizens comprehensive civil, political, human and political rights. In practice, however, there are substantial barriers to realising these rights.

Meeting Basic Needs

The second level in our framework of social justice is the principle that all citizens should be able to meet their basic needs. The welfare state in Britain was founded on a determination to meet the basic needs of all citizens by attacking the 'five great evils' of want, ignorance, squalor, disease and idleness. In Britain fifty years ago, these needs were obvious and manifold:

● In 1940 infant mortality was 56 per 1000. Today the figure is 7.9.

● In 1951, 38 per cent of all houses had no bath. Today, 99 per cent of houses have a bath, and only 38 per cent have no video (which would not be generally regarded as a 'basic need').

● In 1950 only 30 per cent of fifteen year olds were at school - compared to over 95 per cent today.

● In 1936, half of those people aged over 65 living in York were in poverty.

Times have changed for the better. But we must still consider whether or not people's 'basic needs' are being met today. To do this we must, of course, decide what we mean by basic needs. It has been argued, for example, that the overarching basic need is for autonomy, the capacity for *choice*. Autonomous citizens are those who can shape their life and determine its course. In order to meet the need for autonomy a citizen must therefore be possessed of the material resources necessary to participate fully in the way of life of society, in other words to be *included* in society. The European Community now uses the term 'social exclusion' instead of poverty. We believe, however, that most people would distinguish between the basic needs for money, shelter, food, education and health, and the wider resources and opportunities required for full autonomy. These basic needs are, of course, the essential foundation of autonomy, but they are not the same as it. We will therefore return to the goal of personal autonomy in the next section on Opportunities and Life Chances. We have deliberately set a low standard for basic needs, in order to examine the extent of genuine material hardship in the UK.

Although a growing majority of people in this society are able to meet their basic needs, there remains a significant minority of the UK population who are not. The material needs outlined below should be the basic rights of citizenship. In a wealthy society, their absence is a dramatic example of social injustice. We have identified five key areas of basic need: money, shelter, food, education and health.

Basic Needs: Money

Many of our basic needs depend on money. Homelessness and poor housing, low educational achievement, inadequate diet, housing problems and ill-health are all closely associated with low income, and therefore with each other. People with an income which is not sufficient to meet their basic needs are in poverty.

In a number of Western countries, the Government or an appropriate independent body sets a 'Minimum Income Standard' against which to judge citizens' incomes and the levels of state benefits. As Professor John Veit Wilson of Newcastle University has argued in a submission to the Commission, a minimum income standard is one which allows a level of participation which no-one should be denied. The British Government's refusal to set such a standard has been deplored by the House of Commons Social Security Select Committee, and the Social Security Advisory Committee.

In the absence of such a minimum income standard, the poverty line is often taken to be the income support level (formerly the supplementary benefit level) or - given how low that level is - some proportion above it. The result, however, of using income support as a poverty line is that whenever benefits are increased in real terms, so is the number of people 'in poverty'.

The graph below shows the trends in the percentage of the population below the supplementary benefit/income support level, those on or below these benefit levels, and those 40 per cent above the line and below, often considered to be on the margins of poverty.

Figure 1: Numbers of People in Poverty in 1979 and 1989

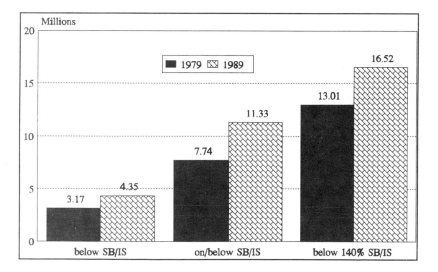

Source: Low Income Statistics: Low Income Families 1979-1989 (Social Security Committee, 1993)

Some of the increase in the proportion living below the different 'poverty levels' is due to small increases in the real level of supplementary benefit/income support over the last ten years. At the same time, however, because benefits were not increased in line with average earnings, the standard of living of people on the lowest incomes actually fell compared with the rest of the population.

It is vital to understand just how basic the income support levels are.

● In 1989 two parents with one child of 10 and another of 14 were expected to live on £90.40 a week, or £4,700 a year. The level today is £115.85 per week, or £6,024 per year.

● In 1989 a single person over 25 was expected to live on £34.90 a week, or £1,815 a year. Today the level is £44.00, or £2,288 per year.

In 1989, 11 million people lived on or below income support levels and 16 million on or below 140 per cent of income support levels. Using the EC measure of poverty (half mean expenditure within each country), the UK witnessed the biggest increase in numbers of poor to the mid-1980s, from below 15 per cent to 20 per cent of the population. Only Portugal, Spain, Ireland and Greece have higher poverty levels. One in five of Europe's poor live in the UK.

Children are particularly affected by poverty. In 1989 the percentage of children in poverty was higher than for the population as a whole; 22 per cent on income support levels or below compared to 20 per cent of the population as a whole. Over three quarters of the children in lone-parent families were living in poverty.

Raw figures like these may not dramatise what it means to live on low income. The 'Breadline Britain' survey by London Weekend Television in 1990 adopted a very simple approach to the measurement of poverty. A MORI poll asked people what items they thought were absolute necessities and then asked whether they themselves had them. The 'absolute necessities' included a bath, telephone and a hobby, but not a car, a night out fortnightly or any friends or family round for a meal. Using this consensual definition of needs, the researchers found that 11 million people lacked three or more of the absolute necessities in 1990, a much higher figure than that found with a similar survey in 1983. This figure of 11 million is the same as that found using the income support level above.

Those most vulnerable to poverty are lone parents, the unemployed, disabled people, pensioners and low-paid workers. More people have been forced to depend on benefits, and the value of benefits compared with earnings has fallen.

● Over the last decade the value of supplementary benefit in relation to earnings fell significantly. Between 1979 and 1991 the value of Supplementary Benefit/Income Support as a proportion of average full-time male earnings fell from 26 per cent to 19 per cent for a married couple and from 16 per cent to 12 per cent for a single person.

Poverty makes it far more difficult and sometimes actually impossible to meet the basic needs for shelter, health, food and education discussed below. It imposes huge demands on people's time, as they struggle with a complex benefits system and substitute their own efforts for services which would cost money. Poverty also restricts access to the credit which most people not in poverty take for granted. Debt hits the poor hardest: on its visits around the country the Commission has been told of loan sharks charging interest of up to 2000 per cent on credit.

The poverty we have discussed so far has been material. But low income can also mean social and emotional poverty. A mother writes;

'We have arguments now, mostly with money - it's all down to lack of money. If we used to get fed up we could go up the street and maybe have a cup of coffee. But now there's no release valve.'

Qualitative academic research reveals similar findings:

'I get so depressed. Kids on at me all the time for this and that, and I know they need it but I just haven't got the money. Then I end up bashing them, then I sit by myself and cry.'

Poverty is also about lack of power, and exclusion:

'Poverty means lack of money. It means lack of ability to do certain things. It means different things to different people. It's about people's power to control what's happening to them'. (Paul, York).

Basic Needs: Shelter

In 1992 there were 140,000 households, (about 400,000 people), officially registered as homeless. The charity Shelter estimate that the true figure is closer to two million. Children are particularly affected.

● During the 1980s the number of homeless households with children rose by 46 per cent. The UK has the fastest rising youth homelessness problem in Europe, with an estimated 150,000 young people becoming homeless each year.

A health care worker in Southampton told the Commission on our visit there that 'the loss of a home is a bereavement as great as any other'. The daily tragedy of homelessness in a wealthy society was graphically related by a young homeless woman. She wrote in her diary:

'Spent the day at the job centre, and went and slept in park all night. 21st birthday.'

Many homeless families are currently living in bed and breakfast accommodation. Carol described to researchers the difference between life in a B&B and shelter in a real home:

'In B&B there was no getting away from a bed. Everything was done on the bed - eating, sleeping, sitting and there was a baby two feet away. You felt under pressure. My nerves were terrible. Whereas when you're in your own place, baby's upstairs in her room. You've got a kitchen to cook in. You've got a table to sit and eat off. You've got a settee to sit and watch TV and a bed to go upstairs to sleep in. It's all completely different.'

As well as the problem of homelessness, there are in Britain today around one and a half million dwellings which are 'unfit for human habitation', according to official definitions. These two groups, those who are homeless or living in inadequate homes, are clearly not having their basic need for shelter met.

But the housing problem does not end there. The dream of owning a home has turned into a nightmare for thousands.

● Mortgage lenders are now the biggest landlords of the potentially homeless; last year 68,540 homes were repossessed.

The basic need for shelter includes the need for warmth and light. In 1991 an estimated 7 million households were unable to keep their home warm, up from 5.5 million in 1981. In 1988 the government reduced fuel payments to low income families by £200 million. The large rises in fuel costs in the 1980s particularly affected low income families.

● The bottom fifth of households in terms of income spend three times as much on fuel as a proportion of their income as the top fifth (though they spend less in absolute terms).

Single pensioners on income support spend 18 per cent their income on fuel. Without adequate compensatory measures, the imposition of VAT on fuel next year will greatly exacerbate the problem of fuel poverty.

Basic Needs: Food

Everyone in Britain should have the resources for an adequate diet. But this basic need is still denied to too many British citizens, selfless parents often sacrificing their own needs for their children.

● A National Children's Home survey of 354 families using NCH centres, of whom 60 per cent were on income support, found that one in five parents had gone hungry in the previous month, half of them so that other members of the family could eat.

As one parent put it to researchers:

'I always try to make sure the kids have something decent ... There have been times when I've had to go without food myself. I haven't liked it but I've known the kids have to be fed. I can go without for a couple of days - they can't.'

In 1991 a couple with one child on income support spent on average £26.16 a week on food, when the minimum cost of a nutritionally health diet was £33.49. Two thirds of parents and over half the children were eating nutritionally poor diets. The National Food Commission states that the cost of an adequate diet in official guidelines is 35 per cent higher than the amount people on low incomes actually spend on food.

Research shows that people on low incomes know what a good diet is - they simply can't afford it. Foods such as chips, chocolate and crisps have more calories per penny than healthier foods, and as one mother put it, 'I have to fill them up'. The cuts in school meal provision have had enormous implications for the diet of children.

● The public service union, NUPE, estimate that in 1980, 40 per cent of a child's daily nutritional requirements were met at school, compared to a figure of 25 per cent today. Between 1979 and 1990 the number of children eating a school lunch fell from 4.9 million to 2.8 million - a drop of 27 per cent.

Provision of clean affordable water to all citizens, whether by a private or public company, is an uncontroversial requirement of any civilised society. In the UK a minority are living without immediate access to clean water. The cost of water has risen on average by 50 per cent (in real terms) in the last five years. This particularly hits low income households, and must be related to the enormous rise in disconnections (177 per cent higher post- than pre-privatisation) discussed below.

Basic Needs: Education

We all have a basic need for an education to equip us for full participation in society. While there has been a secular increase in educational achievement since the Second World War, we do not as a society provide everyone with the foundation of a good basic education.

The benefits of pre-school education have been so well documented that it might reasonably be considered as a basic need in a wealthy country. In France, where over 90 per cent of children attend the *ecoles maternelles*, it is treated as such. In Britain, however, pre-school education has never been compulsory or widely available. We will therefore return to it in the next section, on wider opportunities, although we think there is a strong case for treating pre-school education as a basic need to which all children should be entitled.

Education during the years of compulsory schooling has been recognised as a basic need throughout this century. But not all British children receive an education which could be regarded as even basically adequate to modern demands. The National Foundation for Educational Research found that the average seven year old in 1991 was reading at the level of the average 6½ year old in 1987. In maths, only 4 per cent of English

15-year-olds, compared with 66 per cent of German 15-year-olds, got the right answer to a standard mathematical problem.

Not all schools are adequately resourced. And not all pupils have equal access to a school. A Department for Education discussion paper admits that the Government's education reforms give schools a financial incentive to exclude pupils who make extra demands on teachers or who might lower the school's overall results. Last year 3,000 pupils were permanently excluded from school (many more were temporarily excluded) and the Department states that 'too many children are excluded from school'. Behind the raw figures there is further cause for concern: black pupils were significantly more likely to be excluded, and 13 per cent of excluded pupils have special educational needs.

Once at school, children need personal attention from a teacher. But average primary class sizes have risen in the last decade.

● Between 1982 and 1991 the percentage of primary school children in classes of less than 20 children fell by almost half, from 20.4 per cent to 11.9 per cent.

Although all children have different needs and talents, some children have what are defined as 'special educational needs'. Unfortunately, provision for them is threatened. In late 1991, 15 per cent of LEAs had made cuts to their special needs budget. In many cases this means that pupils are less likely to be educated in mainstream schools; 50 per cent of LEAs reported an increase in the number of pupils placed in special schools. This indicates a reversal of the trend towards greater integration since the mid-1970s.

Our failure as a society to meet basic educational needs is perhaps most graphically illustrated by the fact that in 1991 one in five 21 years olds was innumerate, and one in seven was illiterate. This is a barrier to individual progress;

> 'I went for a job as an ambulance driver and the writing and spelling let me down on it. It stops me getting a better job, a more secure one.'

Lack of basic skills also costs British companies an estimated £5 billion every year, for example because of clerical errors or cancelled orders.

Once at work, it is clear that those with the least education at school get few second chances. Training is diverted to those with the highest initial qualifications, while the six million adults with basic problems in literacy and numeracy are denied opportunities to make up for lost time.

● In 1991, 27 per cent of professionals had received some job related training in the previous four weeks, compared to 3 per cent of unskilled workers.

The reality is that most citizens of the UK do have access to a school and teacher during the years of compulsory schooling. But for those who leave school without the most basic skills or qualifications, not even the right to a basic education is being met. Furthermore, as we will see when we discuss opportunities and life-chances below, this minimum level is inadequate for any society aspiring to extend social justice.

Basic Needs: Health

We are fortunate to live in a country where standards of health and levels of life-expectancy are increasing. For example, average life expectancy rose by two years between 1981 and 1991, infant mortality continues to fall and preventable diseases have been virtually eradicated. But once again, a minority is denied a basic need.

People's health is profoundly affected by their income, housing conditions, environment and diet; it is secured primarily through preventive or public health initiatives rather than through the treatment of illness. In this section our focus is on such measures, although access to basic medical care is also considered.

Preventable diseases, such as dysentery and pleurisy and are rare in modern UK society. There are, however, some disturbing trends which indicate that recently the trend towards eradication has been reversed. The rise in dysentery in England and Wales has been linked to the rise in water disconnections, which are illegal in Scotland. The graph opposite shows the trends in reported cases of dysentery and water disconnections.

Pleurisy rates have also risen from a low of 75 per 100,000 in 1986 to 139 in 1991, a rise of 85 per cent.

Figure 2: Domestic Water Disconnections and Rates of Dysentery

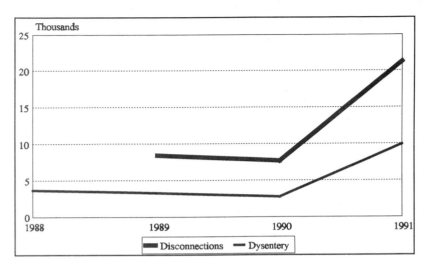

Source: OFWAT May 1993 and Hansard Vol 219 Cols 418W and 473W (Feb 1993)

A dramatic picture of our failure as a society to meet all basic health needs is provided by a startling regional inequality;

● A child born in the West Midlands is three times more likely to die before reaching the age of one *day* than a child in East Anglia.

What matters here is not simply the risk of losing a child, but the fact that basic health needs are not equally met in different parts of the country.

A recent report found that 14,000 babies in need of special care were competing for 800 special care beds. Two thirds of these were paid for by charities.

Preventive health measures can be relatively straightforward and can often actually save money. But the number of people taking an eye-test, which had been rising steadily, fell by 37 per cent when charges were introduced in 1989. Not only are people at risk of not having eyesight problems corrected, they may have undiagnosed neurological problems, which could be picked up at an early stage by opticians.

Commercialisation of dental care also means that access to a dentist offering NHS services can be extremely limited.

● According to the Family Health Services Authority, 98 per cent of dentists in Huntingdon refuse to register patients for NHS care. Between July 1992 and April 1993 dentists in the UK de-registered 440,000 patients.

Opportunities and Life-Chances

As we have seen, most people are able to meet their basic needs at most stages of their lives. But social justice is about far more than basic needs. This section will demonstrate how at the third level in our conceptual framework - concerning opportunities and life-chances - the UK falls far short of a socially just ideal. We remain a society deeply divided in terms of opportunities and life-chances. In contrast to basic needs which are denied only to a minority, the opportunities which make social justice real - above all the opportunities necessary for individuals to develop their talents to the full - are not open to the majority of people. In this section, therefore, we will be examining who has access to which opportunities and how the development of talent and potential is being blocked.

Our survey of life chances reveals that opportunities are too often distributed not on the basis of ability, but of ability to pay; not on who you are but who your parents were; not on what you can offer but on where you live; not on the basis of merit, but on grounds of race or gender. This is what the 6th form students whom we met at a Birmingham secondary school had in mind when, with only one exception, they said that Britain was an unfair society - and that the first unfairness came from class. We now examine five key areas to show how the life chances of people in Britain today are blocked; education and training, employment, good health, a safe environment and financial independence.

Lifelong Learning

Educational attainment has never been as important as it is today. We therefore begin our survey of opportunities and life-chances with education and training - and their potential to equip people with the skills and confidence to shape their own lives. The choices people make, and the opportunities they are offered, before, during and after their schooling have an enormous impact on their later life chances.

British children start compulsory schooling earlier than in many other European countries and the period of compulsory attendance lasts longer than in most of them as well. Yet most will probably spend fewer years in full-time education than young people in a country like France or Sweden, and the majority will attain lower qualifications.

Access to pre-school education and to day care are extremely limited in the UK.

 Less than 8 per cent of British children under the age of 5 have access to registered daycare.

Along with Portugal, the UK has the lowest level of educational provision for under-fives in the EC. Only one in three British 3 and 4-years olds has access to a publicly funded nursery place. In France, the figure is 95 per cent. There are also wide regional variations in the provision of pre-school education.

 In Cleveland, 57 per cent of under-fives are in nursery schools and a further 34 per cent in primary classes, while in Bromley these figures are only 2 per cent and 15 per cent.

Pre-school education is a powerful predictor of future educational achievement, and the educational and social benefits have been shown to extend well into adulthood. The most recent definitive study, in the US, found that every $1000 invested in pre-school education saved the state over $4000 (at the same prices) in benefits, court time and taxes in later years.

A recent comparison by the independent National Institute for Economic and Social Research of qualification levels among 16 to 18 year olds showed France, Germany and Japan performing significantly better than either England or Scotland: seven out of ten pupils in English schools fail to pass three core subjects at age 16. The report found that:

> 'The overall standards of attainment among 16-19 year olds in Britain are significantly lower than in Germany, France and Japan. While the top 20 per cent of attainers do as well as in any country, a much lower proportion of the rest achieve given standards in core areas of general education or in vocation skills ... despite a steady rate of improvement in qualification levels ... The inescapable conclusion is that despite ...

producing a highly qualified elite, Britain is under-performing in the education of the majority of its young people'.

The UK education system is based on failure and not achievement, designed to weed out the majority of pupils from the prestigious academic A-level track. The polarisation of educational paths, between the academic (seen as high risk and only for those who have the highest qualifications) and the vocational (considered as lower status), has a strong influence on this division. Although the proportion of 16-18s in full-time education and training has passed 50 per cent for the first time, this remains one of the lowest participation rates in the industrialised world.

● By the age of 18, only one-quarter of people in Britain are still in full-time education, compared with over 60 per cent in Japan and France.

The graph below compares the UK education record with other industrialised countries.

Figure 3: International Educational Standards

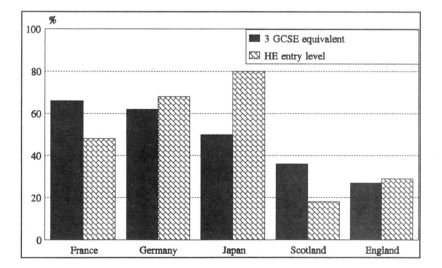

Source: Green and Steedman 1993

Opportunities in education after 16 differ according to social class, ethnicity and region. Participation rates are much higher in private schools; children from the highest occupational group are about twice as likely to remain in education as those from the lowest group; and universities continue to be the destination of a disproportionately high number of children from advantaged home and school backgrounds. For example, 41 per cent of men with fathers from social class I have a degree or equivalent, compared to 5 per cent of men with fathers from social class V. Regional inequalities are also striking; only 4 per cent of women living in Yorkshire and Humberside have a degree or equivalent.

Although independent schools educate only about 7 per cent of pupils they eventually account for over half of all pupils with at least 3 A-Levels (or their equivalent). Private education in the UK is significantly better-resourced than the public sector, with many fewer pupils for each teacher and an astonishing fivefold advantage in terms of capital spending per pupil.

As the table below shows, simplistic assumptions about the educational outcomes of different racial groups no longer apply; white children are least likely to be in post-16 education, followed by Afro-Caribbeans. The highest staying on rates are among Chinese, African Asian and African children. These differences cut across class, so that most ethnic minority children from manual backgrounds have at least the same likelihood of staying in education as most white children from non-manual backgrounds.

Table 1: Still at School: 16-19-year olds in Education by Race - 1990

%	All	Male	Female
Chinese	77	*	*
African	71	*	*
African Asian	66	75	56
Indian	58	55	61
Pakistani	55	64	45
Bangladeshi	46	41	*
AfroCaribbean	43	39	48
White	37	36	38
Other/mixed	58	55	62
All origins	39	38	40
* *sample size too small*			

Source: Britain's Ethnic Minorities (Policy Studies Institute, 1993)

In spite of rising levels of achievement across the population which have seen women close the historical gap on men, there are still important differences between the sexes. Girls and boys continue to be channelled towards different subject choices which offer different career prospects, and girls remain less likely than boys to achieve an A-level pass.

Educational choice should be based on young people's interests and abilities; educational attainment should be reflected in career opportunities and pay. Instead, those who do participate in vocational training might well conclude that training simply doesn't pay. National Vocational Qualifications achieved at Level II can be expected, across a lifetime, to lead to lower earnings than GCSEs which are to be regarded as equivalent. Youth Training Schemes appear to offer even fewer opportunities in this respect.

● In the same job, earnings for those completing a relevant YTS programme were after two years up to 15 per cent lower for both sexes than among those *without* such training.

Similar arguments can be made for adults. Because education is expected to end at age 16, learning becomes a lottery which people take part in for only a small part of their life. A culture of low expectations is the symptom and cause of poor performance.

● Two-thirds of British workers have no vocational or professional qualification, compared with only one quarter of the German workforce.

Of course, training can be demoralising and unproductive unless there is a job at the end of it. As one from Northern Ireland trainee put it to us:

'I'm fed up with training. I feel like a boxer who has been training for five or six years but never gets in the ring. You train and train and yet you're not trained for anything in particular.'

It is to the issue of employment therefore that we now turn.

Work

Paid or unpaid work has a value in and of itself, as an important source of personal identity. And fairly paid work is the most secure and sustainable route out of poverty. In our second discussion paper, we consider in more detail the distribution of paid and unpaid work between women and men, and across people's lifetimes. Here, we focus on paid employment and look at how people enter (or fail to enter) employment; what opportunities people have to move into better jobs; what rights people have in employment, and what the risks are of unemployment.

Access to secure and well-paid jobs is affected by race, class and gender. If we compare people who have the same level of qualifications, we find large, and unjust, differences in their chances of getting a good job.

● White people with at least an A-Level or equivalent are 14 per cent more likely than equally well-qualified Afro-Caribbeans to join the top two occupational groups, and 5 per cent less likely to join the semi/unskilled groups.

Parental occupation is an important influence on work opportunities. Although social mobility has increased along with the number of white-collar jobs, over half the children of working class parents will themselves remain in working-class jobs.

The labour market in Britain (and in most other industrialised countries) has changed dramatically. From a workforce which was mainly male, and substantially employed in manufacturing industry, we now have a workforce which is very nearly half women and substantially employed in services. One in four workers in the UK is now in part-time employment, and 80 per cent of these are women. Women continue to have access to a narrower range of job opportunities than men, beyond a small core of 'high-flyers' who have reached top job posts.

● The civil service now consists of over 50 per cent women. But three-quarters of the lowest grade positions are filled by women, compared with only 6 per cent of the top grade.

Unemployment locks people out of the informal networks through which work opportunities are generated. But the risk of unemployment does not fall equally: those with no qualifications or with few employment skills are far more likely to become unemployed. Men are more likely to be (officially) unemployed than women; younger people and those in their 50's and early 60's are far more likely to be unemployed than those in between; and members of ethnic minority communities are generally more likely to be unemployed than white people.

● In 1992, an unskilled manual worker was five times more likely to be unemployed than a professional.

● In a South Glamorgan survey white Employment Training trainees were 50 per cent more likely to get a job on leaving the scheme than black trainees.

● Pakistanis who worked in non-manual jobs showed an unemployment rate of 13 per cent, compared with 7 per cent among Afro-Caribbeans and 3 per cent among whites in those positions. Bangladeshis in manual jobs were almost three times more likely to lose them than Chinese, African Asian or white manual workers.

The graph below shows unemployment levels for different racial groups with A levels or equivalent.

Figure 4: Unemployment and Race

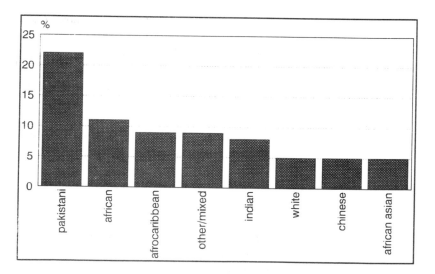

Source: Britain's Ethnic Minorities (Policy Studies Institute, 1993)

Disabled people also have a much higher unemployment rate than non-disabled people. One member of the Glasgow Coalition for Disabled People expressed the point graphically: 'Every time another job loss is announced on the news, disabled people move another place back in the jobs queue'. Unemployment among disabled people is estimated to be around 40 per cent.

Against this background, there is increasing evidence of a more fundamental detachment of a group of unemployed people from those in work and those unemployed for a short time. Long-term unemployment, of over a year's duration, locks people out of the income and routine of a job, but also the usual means of finding employment. In the pre-retirement age group, around half of all unemployed people have been out of work for over a year, compared with a quarter in the youngest age group.

● The long term unemployed are four times less likely to find a job in the following three months than someone becoming unemployed for the first time.

There are stark regional differences in the depth of unemployment. In East Anglia, 24 per cent of the unemployed have been on the dole for more than a year, compared to 54 per cent in Northern Ireland.

A recent trend has been identified which underlines again how official unemployment figures fail to capture the scale of joblessness. Unemployment usually refers to those who are 'economically active'. Traditionally this excludes pensioners, children, students and those who do not register as available for work. It is this last category which has shown a large increase since the mid-1980s:

● Two million men of working age are now no longer actively seeking work, in addition to the 1.7 million registered unemployed.

Life chances are restricted not only by the reality of injustice demonstrated here, but by fear and insecurity. Opinion poll evidence is an imperfect source of information but it provides clues to the mood of the public. Recent survey evidence reveals that between 40 per cent and 50 per cent of those in work are scared of losing their job, with professional workers, manual workers and those in part-time jobs sharing the sense of unease. There is little doubt that such insecurity affects people's behaviour. And there can be no more striking illustration of the extent of social injustice in the UK today - with all its consequences for the decisions made at age 16 - than the finding that today's school age children fear not getting a job more than anything else. According to a Gallup survey, between 40 per cent and 50 per cent of young adults think they will have to wait at least six months after leaving school before they find a job.

Government measures to deregulate the labour market and the shift of power away from collective employee rights towards management prerogatives have made individual employees increasingly insecure.

● The National Association of Citizens' Advice Bureaux point to a consistent pattern where women of less than two years' service are dismissed when they become pregnant.

● Civil service unions report that, faced with competition by external contractors who can undercut wages and conditions, fearful employees are asking how they can sacrifice maternity leave, pension schemes and other rights in a desperate bid to keep their jobs.

Good Health

The World Health Organisation has declared that 'everyone should have the opportunity to attain their health potential'. This implies something far more than the meeting of basic needs, and will obviously vary between countries. But it raises important aspects of personal and collective responsibility for health care and the promotion of good health. Ill-health is often incurable - but it can sometimes be prevented.

The links between poverty and ill-health are well-documented and are explored here. However, new evidence from Richard Wilkinson, of Sussex University, suggests that in advanced industrialised countries it is the *relative* level of income inequality which has the most effect on health, rather than the absolute numbers in poverty. It is estimated that a reduction in inequality would benefit the bottom two thirds of society in terms of life expectancy.

● If income inequality in the UK was reduced to continental levels, we could expect average life expectancy to rise by 2 years.

Infant mortality rates continue to show strong social class and regional biases, although the significant divide now appears to be between groups

D and E (8.3 and 11.2 deaths per thousand respectively) and all other occupational groups (between 5.3 and 6.5 deaths per thousand children).

Life expectancy is clearly related to socio-economic status.

● In Sheffield and Glasgow those who live in the most affluent communities can expect to live eight years longer than those in the most deprived areas.

The impact of unemployment on health is also clear. Unemployed women and men are 30 per cent more likely than the population as a whole to face a chronic long-standing illness or disability. Unemployment can also result in suicide.

● Studies in Edinburgh and Oxford estimate that the attempted suicide rate for unemployed men is between ten and fifteen times higher than among men in work.

Good health is also about freedom from long-standing illnesses. For most chronic illnesses and disabilities, unskilled manual groups are significantly more at risk than those in professional occupations, although it is also worth noting that the prevalence of sickness is relatively high in general, with between 26 per cent and 36 per cent of the adult population reporting some long-standing illness. The UK figure for working time lost through illness or injury is the second highest in the European Community.

The UK's health opportunities reflect how the system of health care operates. One specific indicator is hospital waiting lists. When compared with the system of private health care, being on a long waiting list clearly narrows health opportunities. But regional variations in waiting for the same type of treatment introduce a further inequality of opportunity. For orthopaedic treatment, for example, which can pre-empt long term problems through early and effective treatment, waiting times for a first outpatient appointment is often more than thirty weeks and reached 104 weeks in the East Birmingham NHS Trust in May 1993.

Safe Environment

A clean and safe environment - local, national and global - is central to our own life chances, and those of future generations. Here we consider the issue of personal safety and security at home, in the work place and in the community.

The effects of crime concern us all, from street theft in the inner city to violence in towns and cities on a Saturday night. And as Chief Inspector Julian Smith of Nottinghamshire police told us; 'you can't put a price on someone's quality of life'. The Director of NACRO, Vivien Stern, pointed out to the Commission that 'social disorder is the price we pay for an unjust society'. We know that most reported crime is committed by young men under the age of 21. We also know that young offenders between 16 and 18 are twice as likely to commit an offence when not in work, education or training.

Crime is on the increase. Comparing 1980 to 1993, the percentage of people who had been the victims of burglary, or knew someone who had been a victim, rose from 24 per cent to 38 per cent. For robbery with violence and mugging, the rise was from 5 per cent to 13 per cent.

● Between 1980 and 1993 the number of people who had no experience of crime fell from 65 per cent to 47 per cent of the adult population.

Those least able to protect themselves against crime are most likely to experience it. Residents in the poorest council estates face a risk of burglary which is nearly three times the national average; the risk of vehicle crime is more than double the national average.

Crime reaches beyond those directly affected. Every time another increase in crime is announced, the fear of crime rises too. This fear of crime inhibits the freedom of movement and action of all our citizens, but especially women, the elderly and the young. A Nottingham survey in 1992 found that the fear of crime was the single most important factor in reducing people's enjoyment of their local area.

One of the 'hidden' ways in which personal safety is threatened comes in the shape of domestic violence. Some children are at risk from abuse by adults; some women are at risk from abuse by their partners. Some estimates suggest that across a lifetime, women face a 1 in 4 chance of being victims of domestic violence and at any point in time in the UK, 10 per cent of women in couples are experiencing such abuse.

Children are more likely to develop their potential if they live in communities which offer safe areas to play in. But one in three children whose parents are in partly skilled or unskilled jobs lacks the sole use of a garden, compared with only one in ten of those with professional parents ; four out of ten of the poorer children, compared with one in four of the better-off families, have no access to a safe play area near their home.

One child in fifteen is killed or injured in a road accident between the ages of 5 and 16. Mortality rates for children involved as pedestrians in traffic accidents is related to some extent to local environmental deficiency/insecurity. Again, the correlation with social class is striking. Children from unskilled households are four times as likely to be killed as children from non-manual backgrounds. Accidents account for most of the regional and class variations in child mortality rates.

Figure 5: Killed by Class: child deaths in traffic accidents by social class

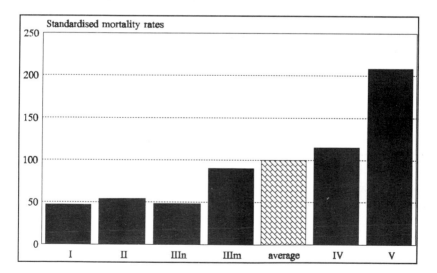

Source: OPCS Occupational Mortality: Childhood Supplement DS No. 8 (1988)

Financial Independence

Financial independence means much more than meeting basic needs. It means security of income at every stage of our lives - during childhood and retirement, as well as during employment or unemployment. It implies that people should not have to fear being unable to make ends meet and should be able to make plans on the basis of a secure income. This section will consider how taxes, benefits, wages, savings and debt influence people's financial independence.

The total tax burden, including expenditure taxes such as VAT as well as income taxes, is greater for the poor than for the rich.

● The top 10 per cent of households pay 32 per cent of their income in tax, compared to 43 per cent for the bottom 10 per cent.

In addition, the marginal rate of taxation for people at the boundary between unemployment and low pay is exceptionally high.

Low pay reduces financial independence; employment is only a pathway out of poverty when it is fairly paid. The abolition of the Wages Councils will further reduce protection against low pay, particularly affecting women - who make up 80 per cent of those covered by the councils.

● An estimated 2.4 million people have earned incomes low enough to qualify them for means-tested benefits such as Family Credit.

The independence women may achieve through employment is also heavily qualified by the gap between their average wages and those of men: despite equal pay legislation, full-time female pay is 78 per cent that of male workers. The effect of a male-oriented labour market and social security system reduce women's capacity to provide for their own retirement.

● On average a man has 41 pensionable years in work; the average woman 24 years (22 years for mothers). Four million women are dependent on pensions derived from their husbands' contributions.

The number of people dependent on income support for long periods indicates how many have no opportunity for financial independence. Two thirds of people on income support have been receiving it for more than a year; 1.7 million claimants, one third of the total, have been on income support for more than three years. Means-tested benefits, originally intended for only rare circumstances, are paying for our failure to extend opportunities for financial independence to all,

Debt crosses the usual income boundaries and affects the ability to plan for the future. Debt-related inquiries to Citizens Advice Bureaux increased by 16 per cent in 1991, twice as fast as other enquiries.

 There are a third of a million families in mortgage arrears and just under two million properties in negative equity. The total value of negative equity is £6 billion, an average of £6,000 for each household affected.

● One in three households with income less than £100 per week have problems with debt.

● Over half the population are unable to save more than £10 a week and/or insure the contents of their home.

Finally, financial insecurity among pensioners and elderly pensioners is growing at the same time as the income of some (particularly younger) pensioners rises.

● 61 per cent of pensioners, particularly those over 70, have an income of less than £5000 a year.

It is the oldest and most vulnerable pensioners who have to rely on the basic state retirement pension and income support in the years when their needs are greatest. Those who are excluded today from employment and contributory pensions may fill their shoes, further widening income inequality in old age.

Unjustified Inequalities

The fourth level in our framework of social justice argues that unfair inequalities of income and wealth are inconsistent with social justice. The issue is not inequalities *per se*: no one believes that absolute arithmetic equality in every sphere is possible or desirable. Some inequalities are indeed justified. The issue here concerns inequalities which are *unjustified* in terms of need, merit or reward. Snapshots of inequality tell us something, but trends are often more revealing. A young volunteer whom we met at the Birmingham Settlement in Newtown, Birmingham, made the point:

'a gap between rich and poor isn't necessarily bad. But when the gap between rich and poor is getting bigger all the time, that's wrong.'

Inequalities in Income

According to government statistics, a high proportion of the population have incomes below the average, which in 1989, at 1992 prices, was £145 a week for a single adult and £395 a week for a couple with three children.

● Almost two-thirds of the population have an income below the average.

The gap between rich and poor fell steadily from the 1940s until the mid- or late-1970s, when this trend towards greater equality, shared across western Europe, was reversed. Income inequality has grown steadily in the 1980s. The graph below shows how income, after tax, was shared out between different groups, from the poorest fifth to the richest fifth between 1977 and 1991. The bottom half of the population now receive only a quarter of the total income, compared to a third in 1979.

Figure 6: The Changing Distribution of Income in the UK*

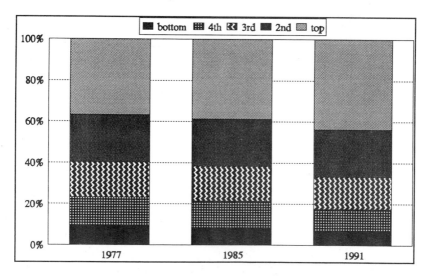

* All figures use the government's equivalence scales, which take account of household size. All figures are after taxation, including indirect taxation, and benefits.
Source: Economic Trends, April 1993 (HMSO)

In 1991, the average annual income of households in the top 20 per cent of the population was £25,320; for the bottom fifth the average was £3,410. If we compare the top and bottom 10 per cent the difference is even more marked: £31,931 and £2,704 per annum, respectively.

The next chart shows the percentage change in the incomes of the bottom half of the population between 1979 and 1991. The average real income (after housing costs) of the bottom tenth fell by 14 per cent, compared to an increase of over 50 per cent for the richest tenth.

Figure 7: Change in Income of Bottom Half of Population 1979-1990/1

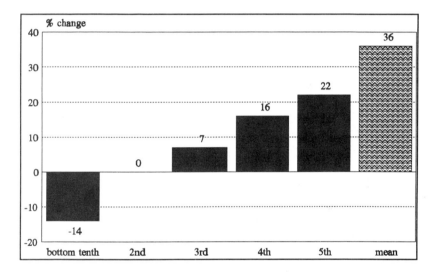

Source: Households Below Average Income: A Statistical Analysis 1979-1990/1
(HMSO 1993)

These figures, from the government's own statistics, show that the gap between rich and poor grew rapidly in the 1980s. While aggregate figures tell us about general trends, we need specific examples to flesh out the statistics and help make judgements about the extent to which inequalities are justified. One such example is the pay of top executives. In the five years to 1992, the pay of the top directors of the FTSE 100 companies rose by 133 per cent, compared to an average increase in earnings of 48 per cent. These large increases in pay of the top executives means that their average salary in 1992 was £535,000 a year, more than £10,000 a week. If their pay had risen at the same pace as the rest of us, they would have been on £334,000.

● The faster rise in the salaries of top executives compared to the average worker has added £200,000 to their pay packet over the last five years.

Figure 8: Directors' Pay - the Growing Gap

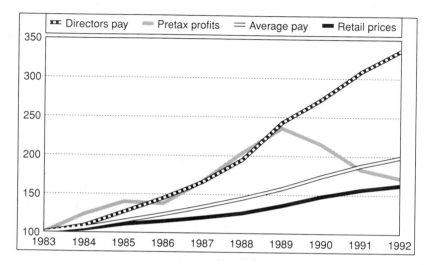

Source: Financial Times/Datastream

Is this necessarily unjust? After all, these executives might deserve these enormous rewards because of the outstanding performance of their companies.

Unfortunately, this is not so. As Figure 8 shows, as pre-tax profits fell after 1988, the pay of directors continued to shoot up. A detailed study of the relationship between executive pay and company performance (measured in terms of returns to shareholders) found that any link between the two disappeared in 1987-88. In other words, the executives getting the biggest rises were not those working for the companies with the best performance. In fact, any association appears to be in the *opposite* direction.

● The highest pay rises in the British corporate sector are not going to those directors with the best company performance; if anything, the opposite is true.

The trend towards greater income inequality is not restricted to the UK; the US and, to a lesser extent, Australia, Canada and Sweden have seen similar shifts. On the other hand, some countries have shown a stable or declining level of inequality, including France, Germany, and Italy. While there are some common economic factors, national polices clearly have a significant impact. The most commonly identified causes of growing inequality in the UK are rising unemployment, increasing wage disparity and changes to the tax and benefits systems. Together these three factors account for most of the change in income inequality. Changes to the tax and benefit system have greatly exacerbated wage inequality and unemployment.

● Of the £31 billion given away in tax cuts between 1979 and 1992, 27 per cent or £8.7 billion went to the top 1 per cent of income earners. £15.2 billion went to the top 10 per cent and 15 per cent or £4.8 billion went to the bottom 50 per cent.

Larger incomes for the rich have not 'trickled down' to those at the bottom. Instead the poorest have got poorer.

Inequalities in Wealth

Those in the higher income groups also own the majority of the country's wealth.

Table 2

The most wealthy	1% of the population own:	18% of all wealth*
"	2% "	25% "
"	5% "	37% "
"	10% "	50% "
"	25% "	71% "
"	50% "	92% "

*Does not include occupational or state pension rights
Source: Inland Revenue Statistics 1993

The composition of wealth has changed over time; property now accounts for over half of all wealth holdings, compared to 20 per cent thirty years ago. The main source of personal wealth remains inheritance, although there has been some decline in its significance.

The pension rights of top directors can place an enormous burden on funds. The large pay rises discussed above will mean that;

● an estimated extra £800 million will have to be paid out of pension funds because of the large pay rises in the 1980s discussed above.

Injustice Today: A Summary

It is important to recognise that standards of living change over time and that the general trend is still towards improvements in living standards for the majority. On average, we are wealthier, healthier, better educated and better housed than we were forty years ago. But too many people are not sharing the benefits. Until the 1980s, inequalities in Britain had been in more or less continuous decline. But this progress was reversed in the last decade, when the absolute income of the poorest 10 per cent of households fell by 6 per cent. These members of our society, who have fallen through an increasingly threadbare safety net, cannot meet their own or their children's basic needs. And for the first time in decades, this minority is growing. This is not, however, the whole story.

Injustice in the UK must be examined according to four standards:

● Formal equality, for example before the law, is accepted in principle but for some people rendered meaningless in practice.

● Basic needs of shelter, nutrition, and education, while now met for the majority of people, are denied to a minority.

● For a large proportion of the population, opportunities are limited and life-chances denied.

● Unjustified inequalities are increasingly evident. Our snapshot of injustice shows there is much work to be done.

In the next part of this report, we suggest an agenda that goes beyond the consolidation of formal rights and the completion of Beveridge's attack on the 'five great evils' he identified fifty years ago. We must of course complete these tasks, but we also need to go further. The widest possible access to opportunities must be extended to all our citizens, and unjustifiable inequalities attacked.

→ welfare

THE NEW AGENDA:
FROM FIVE GREAT EVILS TO FIVE GREAT OPPORTUNITIES

The contemporary context for the debate about social justice is very different from that of the 1940s, which provided the backdrop for the deliberations of the Beveridge Committee.

● Beveridge took for granted that while the welfare state would be *(1)* needed for the temporary relief of unemployment, Keynesian demand management would maintain high and stable employment.

● Beveridge took for granted a stable and nuclear family structure, founded on the paid employment of a male breadwinner, and the *(2)* unpaid caring work of women.

● Above all, the Beveridge plan took for granted the common national purpose of economic and social reconstruction - a sound basis for *(3)* a thoroughgoing attack on the 'five great evils of want', disease, ignorance, squalor and idleness.

The Commission on Social Justice can make none of these assumptions. Keynesian demand management is plainly not enough to guarantee high employment in a world of global competition and capital flows; the nuclear family is no longer the universal household unit, and women now make up almost half the labour force; finally, and perhaps most profoundly, there is ideological and political confusion about objectives and strategies for public policy.

In contrast to Beveridge, and partly as a result of the successes of his innovations, the Commission on Social Justice cannot assume ideological consensus about the objectives for public policy. Whereas Beveridge set out to establish for all citizens a minimum floor of rights to income, health, housing, and education, our task today is more complex and in some ways more ambitious. Social progress has raised political sights, and paradoxically generated political division.

Our conception of social justice outlined in Part 2 of this document proceeded from a simple idea of the equal worth of all citizens to radical conclusions, about the ability of all citizens to meet basic needs, the extension of opportunities and life-chances, and the elimination of unjustifiable inequalities. In contrast to Beveridge, we go further than an attempt to meet minimum rights of citizenship: in effect, we say that these minimum rights are necessary but by no means sufficient for a socially just society. In our hierarchy of ideas of social justice, the satisfaction of basic needs gets us to level two: but the furtherance of social justice demands more.

The evidence of Part 3 of this report - the 'Map of Injustice' - is that in numerous ways, social injustice dogs British society, but the injustices are different from the evils identified by Beveridge fifty years ago. In the terms of our framework for social justice, and notwithstanding the many problems that still exist, a summary report would therefore conclude that; the formal foundations of citizenship are in place; Beveridge's project of meeting basic needs has been started but not completed; the radical agenda for the extension of opportunities has a long way to go; and the reduction of unjustifiable inequalities has been reversed in recent years.

For Beveridge, the primary goal was the elimination of five great evils; and his project must be completed. But the Commission on Social Justice wants to raise the sights of public policy, by moving forwards from the 'five great evils' to the 'five great opportunities' that will in the years ahead be the basis of social cohesion and economic security. These opportunities - for lifelong learning, work, good health, a safe environment and financial independence - are today's political and moral frontier.

Lifelong Learning

We have seen in Part 3 of this report how opportunities for education and training are limited for millions of people. Over the next year we will be seeking new ways to extend opportunity to those denied the services and resources needed to develop their talents to the full. After two centuries in which the social value of education has been at the heart of progressive politics, economic need now also requires that the full fruits of learning be extended across the whole population.

Work

Work is central to personal identity and national progress. Today, we face new demands for skill, application and care, and it must be a central tenet of a socially just society that all its citizens are given the opportunity to give of their best through both paid employment and unpaid work. While for much of this century the relationship between the two has been considered unproblematic - men worked for money, women for love - that is no longer the case. The problems of employment, and the unmet needs for care, require us to confront the issue of how paid and unpaid work is distributed between men and women, and across people's lives.

Good Health

Fifty years ago, Beveridge conceived of the health service as a sickness service, free at the point of use and the time of need. Today, the 'points of use' are all around us -we all breathe common air and drink common water - and the 'times of need' are not intermittent but ongoing. 'Avoidable' deaths are more the result of failure of early diagnosis than lack of final care; 'accidental deaths' - in house fires or traffic accidents - are correlated to class position; and average life expectancy has been linked not to national income or poverty but to relative inequalities. The promotion of good health - perhaps the most fundamental aspect of human autonomy - is not a matter for a sickness service, but for all aspects of government policy. The opportunity to enjoy good health is fundamental to social justice, but it is a collective as well as individual responsibility.

Safe Environment

Central to anyone's life-chances is the personal security of their environment - at home, at work and in the community. The fear of crime or injury is both intensely personal and by definition communal: it blights communities and households, as well as the lives of individuals. We are social beings, and if society is unsafe, we cannot realise our own potential within it. At a global level, environmental degradation threatens the wellbeing of future generations as well as ourselves.

Financial Independence

While freedom from want is a basic need, the opportunity to enjoy financial independence is a more radical demand for social justice.

Financial independence for women and men involves more than the ability to earn a living, to save and to build up assets; it requires a dependable income at every stage of life, including periods spent in unpaid work.

To supplement the attack on the evils highlighted by Beveridge, the Commission will, in the next phase of our work, be directing our attention to this new agenda, an agenda of opportunity, where the fulfilment of potential and development of talent mark a new phase in social and economic progress.

REFERENCES AND FURTHER READING

Ideas of Social Justice

Dworkin R (1981) 'What is Equality? Part 1: Equality of Welfare', and 'What is Equality? Part 2: Equality of Resources'. *Philosophy and Public Affairs* 10.

Hayek F A (1976) *Law, Legislation and Liberty Volume 2: The Mirage of Social Justice* (London: Routledge and Kegan Paul).

Miller D (1992) 'Distributive Justice: What the People Think'. *Ethics* 102 (April).

Nozick R (1974) *Anarchy, State and Utopia.* (Oxford: Blackwell).

Nussbaum M and Sen A K (eds) (1992) *The Quality of Life* (Oxford: OUP).

Rawls J (1971) *A Theory of Justice* (Oxford: OUP).

---------- (1992) *(Political Liberalism* (Oxford: OUP).

Sen A K (1992) *Inequality Re-examined* (Cambridge, Mass: Harvard University Press).

Titmuss R (1971) *The Gift Relationship: from Human Blood to Social Policy* (New York).

Walzer M (1983) *Spheres of Justice* (Oxford: Blackwell).

A New Map of Injustice

Equal Worth

H M Government (1992) *1991 Census* (HMSO).

Hodgson G (1993) *The Electoral Register: A Squinting Eye to Democracy* (London: Charter 88).

Law Society Briefing (1993) *Lord Chancellor's Legal Aid Proposals: debate on Lord Irvine's motion* (London: Law Society).

NACRO (1993) *Criminal Justice Digest*, January 1993 (London: NACRO).

Basic Needs

Constantine S (1983) *Social Conditions in Britain 1918-1939* (London: Methuen).

Money:

Barnardo's (1990) *Missing the Target* (London: Barnardo's).

London Weekend Television (1991) *Breadline Britain 1990s* (London: LWT).

Oppenheim C (1993) *Poverty: the facts* (London: CPAG).

Wilson J V (1993) *Why Social Justice requires Governments to Promote and Use Minimum Income Standards* (unpublished submission).

Shelter:

Boardman B (1991) *Ten Years Cold: lessons from a decade of fuel poverty* (Newcastle: Neighbourhood Energy Action).

Central London Social Security Advisers Forum (1989) *One day I'll have my own place to stay* (London: CLSSAF).

Crane H (1990) *Speaking from Experience* (London: Bayswater Hotel Homeless Project).

Department of the Environment (1993) *1991 English House Conditions Survey* (London: HMSO).

Hutton S (1993) *Assessing the impact of the imposition of VAT on fuel on low income households: analysis of the fuel expenditure data from the 1991 Family Expenditure Survey* (York: Social Policy Research Unit).

Scottish Anti-Poverty Network (1993) *Fuel Poverty Factsheet* (Glasgow: SAPN).

Food:

Dibb S (Forthcoming) *Food, Low Income Families and School Meals* (London: Family Policy Studies Centre).

National Children's Home (1991) *Poverty and Nutrition Survey* (London: NCH).

NUPE (1992) *School Meals Factfile No. 1* (London: NUPE).

Education:

Adult Literacy and Basic Skills Unit (1987) *Literacy, Numeracy and Adults: evidence from the National Child Development Study* (London: ALBSU).

---------- (1993) *The Cost to Industry: basic skills and the UK workforce* (London: ALBSU).

---------- (1993) *The Basic Skills of Young Adults* (London: ALBSU).

Department for Education (1992) *Exclusions: a discussion paper* (London: DFE).

Department of Employment (1991) *Training Statistics 1991* (London: HMSO).

Green F (1993) *The skills problem and inequality in training* (IPPR seminar, May).

Mortimore P (1993) *The issue of class size* (London: National Commission on Education Briefing Paper No. 12).

Wedell K (1993) *Special Needs Education: the next 25 years* (London: National Commission on Education Briefing Paper No. 14).

Health:

Cambridgeshire Family Health Services Authority (1992) *Access to NHS Dentistry* (Cambridge: letter, December).

Federation of Ophthalmic and Dispensing Opticians (1992) *Optics at a Glance* 1992 (London: FODO).

Institute of Environmental Health Officers (1992) *Disconnections of Domestic Water Supplies* (London: IEHO).

OPCS (1990) *DH6 No.4* (London: HMSO).

Opportunities and Life-Chances

Lifelong Learning:

Bennett R, Glennerster H and Nevison D (1991) *Learning should pay* (London: BP/London School of Economics).

Berrueta-Clement (1984) *Changed Lives: the effect of the Perry pre-school programmes on youths through age 19* (Monographs of the High/Scope Educational Research Foundation No. 8).

Cohen B and Fraser N (1991) *Childcare in Modern Welfare System: Towards a new national* (London: IPPR).

Department for Education (1993) *Pupils under five years in age in schools in England and Wales* (London: DFE Statistical Bulletin Issue No 11/93).

H M Government (1991) *General Household Survey* (London: HMSO).

---------------------- (1990) *Labour Force Survey* (London: HMSO).

Green A and Steedman H (1993) *Educational provision, educational attainment and the needs of industry: a review of research for Germany, France, Japan, the USA and Britain* (London: National Institute for Economic and Social Research, report Series No. 5).

Green F (1993) *The skills problem and inequality in training* (IPPR seminar, May).

Jones T (1993) *Britain's Ethnic Minorities* (London: Policy Studies Institute).

Raffe D (1992) *Participation of 16-18 year olds in education and training* (London: National Commission on Education Briefing No. 3).

School Examination Survey (1992)) *Statistical Bulletin* (London: 15/92).

Work:

Curtice J and Gallagher T (1990) 'The Northern Irish Dimension' in Roger Jowell *et al* (eds) *British Social Attitudes: The 7th report* (Aldershot: Gower).

Financial Times (1993) 'Sharp rise in job fears among professionals and managers' (1 June).

GALLUP (1993) *Youth Survey* (London: GALLUP).

National Association of Citizens Advice Bureaux (1992) *Not in Labour: CAB evidence on pregnancy, dismissal and employment* (London: NACAB).

Ogbonna E (1992) *Ethnic Minorities, Employment Training and Business Start-up Schemes* (Cardiff: Cardiff Business School).

Philpott J (1993) *Equality and Efficiency: the incidence and cost of unemployment* (IPPR seminar, May).

Good Health:

Blunkett D (1993) *The waiting list the government would like to hide* (Press Release 10 May).

H M Government (1991) *General Household Survey 1991* (London: HMSO).

OPCS (1990) *DH3 and DH6* (London: HMSO).

Townsend P, Davidson N and Whitehead M (1992) *Inequalities in Health* (London: Penguin).

Whitehead M (1990) *The Concepts and Principles of Equity in Health* (Geneva: World Health Organisation).

Wilkinson R (1992) 'Income Distribution and Life Expectancy", *British Medical Journal* (Vol 304).

Financial Independence:

Equal Opportunities Commission (1992) *Women and Men in Britain* (London: HMSO).

H M Government (1993) *Economic Trends* January 1993, May 1993 (London: HMSO).

Scottish Low Pay Unit (1993) *Women to suffer under Wages Council abolition,* Payline No.12 (Glasgow: SLPU).

Smith S (1991) *Economic Policy and the Division of Income within the Family* (London: Institute for Fiscal Studies).

Safe Environment:

GALLUP (1993) *Crime and Punishment* (London: GALLUP Report 393).

GALLUP (1993) *Youth Survey* (London: GALLUP).

Home Office (1992) *Research Findings Bulletin,* October.

Philpott J (1993) *Equality and Efficiency: The incidence and cost of unemployment* (IPPR seminar, May).

OPCS (1990) *Occupational Mortality: Childhood Supplement DS no. 8* (London: HMSO).

Townsend P (1979) *Poverty in the United Kingdom* (London: Penguin).

Unjustified Inequalities

Atkinson A (1993) *What is happening to the distribution of income in the UK?* (London: LSE Welfare State Programme No. 87).

H M Government (1993) *Economic Trends May 1993 - Effect of Taxes and Benefits upon Household Income* (London: HMSO).

Gregg P *et al* (1993) *The Disappearing Relationship Between Directors' Pay and Company Performance* (London: London School of Economics Centre for Economic Performance Working Paper No. 282).

Inland Revenue (1993) *Statistics 1993* (London: HMSO).

Johnson P and Webb S (1993) 'Explaining the Growth in UK Income Inequality: 1979-1988/9', *The Economic Journal* 103, March.

Laurence B (1993) 'Timebomb ticks under boardroom bonanza' (*Guardian* May 22).

Oppenheim C (1993) *Poverty: The Facts* (London, CPAG).

Department of Social Security (1993) *Households Below Average Income: A Statistical Analysis 1979 - 1990/1* (London: HMSO).

THE COMMISSION ON SOCIAL JUSTICE
Terms of Reference

The Commission on Social Justice was set up with the following terms of reference:

● To consider the principles of social justice and their application to the economic well-being of individuals and the community;

● To examine the relationship between social justice and other goals, including economic competitiveness and prosperity;

● To probe the changes in social and economic life over the last fifty years, and the failure of public policy to reflect them adequately; and to survey the changes that are likely in the foreseeable future, and the demands they will place on government;

● To analyse public policies, particularly in the fields of employment, taxation and social welfare, which could enable every individual to live free from want and to enjoy the fullest possible social and economic opportunities;

● And to examine the contribution which such policies could make to the creation of a fairer and more just society.

Membership

The 16 members of the Commission on Social Justice are:

Sir Gordon Borrie (Chairman)	Former Director-General of Fair Trading
Professor A B Atkinson, FBA	Professor of Political Economy, University of Cambridge.
Anita Bhalla	Treasurer, Asian Resource Centre, Birmingham.
Professor John Gennard	Professor of Industrial Relations, University of Strathclyde.
Very Rev John Gladwin	Provost, Sheffield Cathedral.
Christopher Haskins	Chief Executive, Northern Foods, PLC.
Patricia Hewitt	Deputy Director, IPPR.
Dr Penelope Leach	President, Child Development Society.
Professor Ruth Lister	Professor and Head of the Deptartment of Applied Social Studies, University of Bradford.
Emma MacLennan	Vice Chair, Low Pay Unit.
Professor David Marquand	Professor of Politics, University of Sheffield.
Bert Massie	Director, Royal Association for Disability and Rehabilitation.
Dr Eithne McLaughlin	Lecturer in Social Policy, Queen's University of Belfast.
Steven Webb	Economist, Institute for Fiscal Studies.
Margaret Wheeler	Director of Organisation Development, UNISON.
Professor Bernard Williams	White's Professor of Moral Philosophy, University of Oxford.

Evidence

The Commission has already received a large number of informal submissions from individuals and organisations about our remit, the problems we must confront, and the strategies we should adopt to solve them. We also know, however, that many people want to submit formal evidence to the Commission, covering their ideas for social reform, economic renewal and political change.

With the publication of our first two discussion documents, of which this is the first, the Commission has completed the first phase of its work - a preliminary ground-clearing and objective-setting exercise. We are now entering phase 2, when we will be looking in some detail at various policy options, and how they can help us realise the objectives set out in this publication. We will over the course of the second half of 1993 and the beginning of 1994 be publishing a series of shorter discussion papers about certain aspects of public policy, and they may provoke further thinking.

We would therefore very much welcome written evidence from any quarter. Oral hearings may be held, but none are yet planned.

Anyone wishing to contact the Commission can do so through either its London or Glasgow office, at the following addresses:

Commission on Social Justice
Institute for Public Policy Research
30-32 Southampton Street
London WC2E 7RA
(tel: 071 379-9400)

Commission on Social Justice
c/o Centre for Housing Research
Glasgow University
25 Bute Gardens
Glasgow G12 8RT
(tel: 041 339-8855 ext.4675)